10 Businesses You can start right now with little or no money!

By Brian Mahoney

Introduction

Welcome to "10 Businesses You can start right now with little or no money!"

While it might seem like hyperbole to say that you could start a business little or no money, when you look at the list of businesses in this book, it's easy to see that's really possible.

For example many people already have paint in their garage and Aliexpress sells airbrushes that start at under $6.00 to get started with a Airbrush Business. Most already own a lawn mower for a lawn care business, cleaning materials for a Foreclosure Cleaning business. Do your own taxes with Turbo Tax or any other tax preparation software, an you don't have to spend a dime to get started with a Tax Preparation business. You get the idea. If you would like some money to start your business, then at the end of each chapter I give you a link for a low cost audiobook you can download instantly to find out how to get massive money for your business.

You can get a website for free & YouTube is still free to join & place videos with info about your business with a link in the video description to send traffic to your website. To learn more "how to"details use the link below.

"How to make money on YouTube"

https://www.amazon.com/dp/1795585439

I currently run several businesses and I can tell you, it's a good feeling having multiple streams of income in good times and trying times.

So get excited! Be ready to take massive action to make your financial dreams come!

Table of Contents

1. Airbrush Business
2. Crochet Business
3. Foreclosure Cleaning Business
4. Gift Basket Business
5. Jewelry Business
6. Lawn Care Business
7. Locksmith Business
8. Animal Care & Pet Sitting Business
9. Tax Preparation Business
10. Vending Machine Business

Copyright © 2020 MahoneyProducts

DEDICATION

This book is dedicated to my sister Rachel
a kind person and a blessing from God.

ACKNOWLEDGMENTS

I WOULD LIKE TO ACKNOWLEDGE ALL THE HARD WORK OF THE MEN AND WOMEN OF THE UNITED STATES MILITARY, WHO RISK THEIR LIVES ON A DAILY BASIS, TO MAKE THE WORLD A SAFER PLACE.

Disclaimer

This book was written as a guide to starting a business. As with any other high yielding action, starting a business has a certain degree of risk. This book is not meant to take the place of accounting, legal, financial or other professional advice. If advice is needed in any of these fields, you are advised to seek the services of a professional.

While the author has attempted to make the information in this book as accurate as possible, no guarantee is given as to the accuracy or currency of any individual item. Laws and procedures related to business are constantly changing.

Therefore, in no event shall Brian Mahoney or MahoneyProducts Publishers be liable for any special, indirect, or consequential damages or any damages whatsoever in connection with the use of the information herein provided.

All Rights Reserved

No part of this book may be used or reproduced in any manner whatsoever without the written permission of the author.

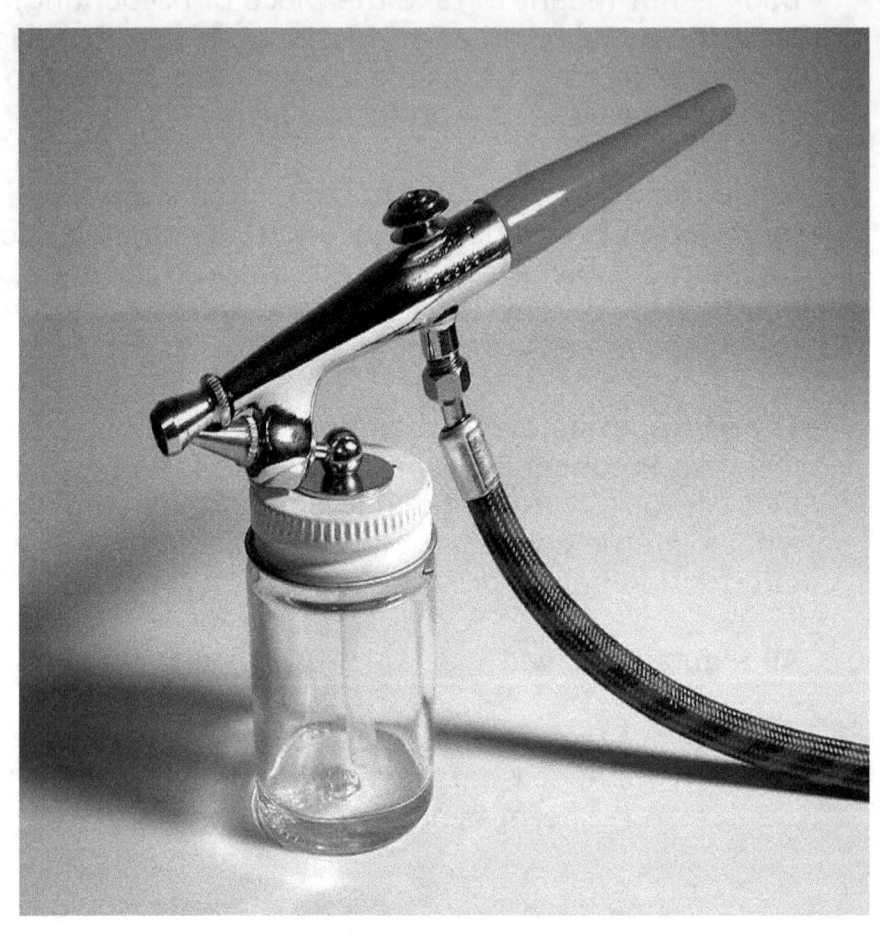

A Paasche F#1 single action external mix airbrush

AIRBUSH BUSINESS

AIRBRUSH BUSINESS OVERVIEW

Airbrush Business

Estimated Yearly Income: $24,000 - $70,000

Startup Costs: $100 - $1,000

Normal fees: $100 - $200 per hour.

Marketing/Advertising: Organic SEO, YouTube, Google Ads, Flyers, art studios, art supply stores, trade and craft shows, business website

Start up Equipment: Airbrush, canvas, cloth, masks, hose

Skills needed: Trained in Graphic design, degree in Art

Home Based: Can be operated from home.

Part Time: Can be operated part-time.

Franchises Available? No

Online Operation? No

AIRBUSH BUSINESS

Paint airbrushing is very popular and has many uses including customizing vehicles, creating murals, decorating clothing, and creating a one-of-a-kind paint finish on almost any product. The equipment necessary for this business is inexpensive and can be ordered through art supply or paint supply stores. I contacted two businesses that offered custom airbrushing services; one advertised in the Yellow Pages and the other was referred to me by an automotive body shop. In both instances, the charge to create custom airbrushed images was $60 per hour (plus materials) with no guarantees on how long it would take to finish the job. Working a mere 25 hours a week at these rates could earn you as much as $70,000 per year.

Airbrush

An airbrush is a small, air-operated tool that sprays various media including ink and dye, but most often paint by a process of nebulization. Spray guns were developed from the airbrush and are still considered a type of airbrush.

Design

An airbrush works by passing a stream of fast moving (compressed) air through a venturi, which creates a local reduction in air pressure (suction) that allows paint to be pulled from an interconnected reservoir at normal atmospheric pressure.

AIRBUSH BUSINESS

The high velocity of the air atomizes the paint into very tiny droplets as it blows past a very fine paint-metering component. The paint is carried onto paper or other surface. The operator controls the amount of paint using a variable trigger which opens more or less a very fine tapered needle that is the control element of the paint-metering component. An extremely fine degree of atomization is what allows an artist to create such smooth blending effects using the airbrush.

Types

Aerograph Super 63, a gravity fed, double action, internal mix airbrush

Airbrushes are usually classified by three characteristics. The first characteristic is the action performed by the user to trigger the paint flow while the second is the mechanism for feeding the paint into the airbrush and the third is the point at which the paint and air mix.

Trigger

The simplest airbrushes work with a single action mechanism where the depression of the trigger actuates air flow through the airbrush. The airbrush's color flow and spray pattern are adjusted separate of the trigger action.

AIRBUSH BUSINESS

Dual action airbrushes (Badger Patriot 105, Paasche VL, Iwata CM-C are all good examples of dual action airbrushes) are of a more sophisticated design model than single action airbrushes, which tends to make them the more expensive of the two.

Feed system

Paint can be fed by gravity from a paint reservoir sitting atop the airbrush (called gravity feed) or siphoned from a reservoir mounted below (bottom feed) or on the side (side feed). Each feed type carries unique advantages. Gravity feed instruments require less air pressure for suction as the gravity pulls the paint into the mixing chamber.

Typically instruments with the finest mist atomization and detail requirements use this method. Side- and bottom-feed instruments allow the artist to see over the top, with the former sometimes offering left-handed and right-handed options to suit the artist. A bottom feed airbrush typically holds a larger capacity of paint than the other types, and is often preferable for larger scale work such as automotive applications and tee-shirt design.

AIRBUSH BUSINESS

Mix point

With an internal mix airbrush the paint and air mix inside the airbrush (in the tip) creating a finer atomized "mist" of paint. With external mix the air and paint exit the airbrush before mixing with each other, which creates a larger coarser atomization pattern. External mix airbrushes are cheaper and more suited for covering larger areas with more viscous paints or varnishes.

Technique

Airbrush technique is the freehand manipulation of the airbrush, medium, air pressure and distance from the surface being sprayed in order to produce a certain predictable result on a consistent basis with or without shields or stencils. Airbrush technique will differ with the type of airbrush being used (single action or dual/double action).

Double action airbrush technique involves depressing the trigger on the top of the airbrush with the index finger to release air only, and drawing it back gradually to the paint release threshold. The most important procedural dynamic is to always begin with air only and end with air only.

AIRBUSH BUSINESS

Single action airbrush technique derives its name from the fact that only one action is required for operation. The single action of depressing the trigger releases a fixed ratio of paint to air. Achieving different line widths requires either changing the tip and nozzle combination or else adjusting the spray volume manually between spray width changes. The most important aspect of proper single action airbrush technique is to keep the hand moving before the trigger is depressed and after the trigger is released. This avoids the "bar bell" line.

Use

* **Murals**

* **Airbrushes are also suitable for painting murals.**

* **Airbrush makeup application**

* **Art and illustration**

* **Photo retouching**

The term "airbrushed" or "airbrushed photo" has also been used to describe glamour photos in which a model's imperfections have been removed.

Using today's digital imaging technology, this kind of picture editing is now usually done with a raster image editor.

AIRBUSH BUSINESS

Airbrushes can also be used to apply:

* Temporary airbrush tattoos.

* Airbrush tanning

* Finger nail art

* Clothing (T Shirts)

* Automotive

* Street artists

Choose the Right Airbrush

Single Action vs. Double Action?

A single action airbrush is the most basic type of airbrush that you can get. When you press down on the control lever (button), the airbrush paint is immediately mixed with the air flow and sprayed out at a pre set rate.

A dual action airbrush set gives you complete control not only of the air flow, but also of the paint flow to the airbrush without the need to stop and make adjustments. A dual action airbrush is the only way to go if you are serious about airbrushing and want to achieve quality, consistent results. There is a reason that professional airbrush artists choose to use dual action instead of single action airbrushes. They're a better airbrush, simple as that.

AIRBUSH BUSINESS

Single action airbrushes are used mostly for activities that do not require a high level of detail or control.

A dual action airbrush set is an absolute necessity for any serious airbrush artist.

Gravity vs. Suction (siphon) Feed?

Suction fed airbrushes work by "sucking" the paint up a hose that is inserted into the paint bottle hanging below the airbrush.

Suction fed airbrushes are very popular for painting t-shirts and other textiles, as these types of paints are usually thicker and spray better with a suction feed airbrush.

Gravity fed airbrushes use a lot less paint than a suction fed airbrush, so making quick color changes is much easier when using a gravity fed brush. These airbrush sets tend to be easier to clean as well, since there are no jars of paint or suction tubes to clean up when finished painting or changing colors.

The choice is yours. Choose your equipment, and business niche and take massive action to be a success with your Airbrush business.

AIRBUSH BUSINESS
Fast Start Web Resource

http://www.aliexpress.com/wholesale/wholesale-airbrush-supplies.html

http://www.dhgate.com/wholesale/airbrush-tattoo-supplies/c018017016.html

http://www.tcpglobal.com/AirbrushDepot/

http://www.jerrysartarama.com/discount-art-supplies/Airbrushing.htm

http://thetanningstore.com/Airbrush-Tanning-Supplies/

http://www.discountairbrush.com/

https://www.coastairbrush.com/

How to get Free Money for Small Business Start up

https://www.amazon.com/dp/1951929144   Paperback

https://urlzs.com/ZamJw   AudioBook

Basic Airbrush Techniques Training Video:

http://www.youtube.com/watch?v=RpSqCr8P1Hs

Crochet Business

Crochet Business Overview

Start-up Cost: $100 - $300
Potential Earnings: $3,000-$10,000

Typical Fees: $5 - $100

Advertising:

Zero Cost Online Marketing, Internet Marketing, Business Cards, Classified Ads, Yellow Pages, Online Yellow Pages, Website, Referrals, Direct Mail Postcards, Business Groups

Qualifications:

Knowledge of Crocheting and Knitting

Equipment Needed:

Needles and crochet hooks, yarn, simple patterns, scissors

Home Business Potential: Yes

Staff Required: No

Hidden Costs:

Insurance & licensing; Fluctuating material costs

Crochet Business

Crochet (English pronunciation: /kroʊˈʃeɪ/; French: [kʁɔʃɛ]) is a process of creating fabric by interlocking loops of yarn, thread, or strands of other materials using a crochet hook. The name is derived from the French term "crochet", meaning small hook. These are made of materials such as metal, wood, or plastic and are manufactured commercially and produced in artisan workshops. The salient difference between crochet and knitting, beyond the implements used for their production, is that each stitch in crochet is completed before proceeding with the next one, while knitting keeps a large number of stitches open at a time. (Variant forms such as Tunisian crochet and broomstick lace keep multiple crochet stitches open at a time.)

Etymology

The word crochet is derived from the Old French crochet, a diminutive of croche, in turn from the Germanic croc, both meaning "hook". It was used in 17th-century French lace making, crochetage designating a stitch used to join separate pieces of lace, and crochet subsequently designating both a specific type of fabric and the hooked needle used to produce it. Although that fabric is not known to be crochet in the present sense, a genealogical relationship between the techniques sharing that name appears likely.

Crochet Business

Crochet has experienced a revival on the catwalk. Christopher Kane's Fall 2011 Ready-to-Wear collection makes intensive use of the granny square, one of the most basic of crochet motifs. In addition, crochet has been utilized many times by designers on the popular reality show Project Runway.

Even websites such as **Etsy** and **Ravelry** have made it easier for individual hobbyists to sell and distribute their patterns or projects across the internet.

Laneya Wiles released a music video titled "Straight Hookin'" which makes a play on the word "hookers," which has a double meaning for both "one who crochets" and "a prostitute."

Materials

Basic materials required for crochet are a hook and some type of material that will be crocheted, most commonly yarn or thread. Additional tools are convenient for keeping stitches counted, measuring crocheted fabric, or making related accessories. Examples include cardboard cutouts, which can be used to make tassels, fringe, and many other items; a pom-pom circle, used to make pom-poms; a tape measure and a gauge measure, both used for measuring crocheted work and counting stitches; a row counter; and occasionally plastic rings, which are used for special projects. In recent years, yarn selections have moved beyond synthetic and plant and animal-based fibers to include bamboo, qiviut, hemp, and banana stalks, to name a few.

Crochet Business

Crochet hook

The crochet hook comes in many sizes and materials, such as bone, bamboo, aluminium, plastic, and steel. Because sizing is categorized by the diameter of the hook's shaft, a crafter aims to create stitches of a certain size in order to reach a particular gauge specified in a given pattern. If gauge is not reached with one hook, another is used until the stitches made are the needed size.

Crafters may have a preference for one type of hook material over another due to aesthetic appeal, yarn glide, or hand disorders such as arthritis, where bamboo or wood hooks are favored over metal for the perceived warmth and flexibility during use. Hook grips and ergonomic hook handles are also available to assist crafters.

Steel crochet hooks range in size from 0.4 to 3.5 millimeters, or from 00 to 16 in American sizing. These hooks are used for fine crochet work such as doilies and lace.

Aluminium, bamboo, and plastic crochet hooks are available from 2.5 to 19 millimeters in size, or from B to S in American sizing.

Artisan-made hooks are often made of hand-turned woods, sometimes decorated with semi-precious stones or beads.

Crochet Business

Crochet hooks used for Tunisian crochet are elongated and have a stopper at the end of the handle, while double-ended crochet hooks have a hook on both ends of the handle. There is also a double hooked apparatus called a Cro-hook that has become popular.

A hairpin loom is often used to create lacy and long stitches, known as hairpin lace. While this is not in itself a hook, it is a device used in conjunction with a crochet hook to produce stitches.

Yarn

Yarn for crochet is usually sold as balls or skeins (hanks), although it may also be wound on spools or cones. Skeins and balls are generally sold with a yarn band, a label that describes the yarn's weight, length, dye lot, fiber content, washing instructions, suggested needle size, likely gauge, etc. It is a common practice to save the yarn band for future reference, especially if additional skeins must be purchased. Crocheters generally ensure that the yarn for a project comes from a single dye lot. The dye lot specifies a group of skeins that were dyed together and thus have precisely the same color; skeins from different dye lots, even if very similar in color, are usually slightly different and may produce a visible stripe when added onto existing work. If insufficient yarn of a single dye lot is bought to complete a project, additional skeins of the same dye lot can sometimes be obtained from other yarn stores or online.

Crochet Business

Process

Crocheted fabric is begun by placing a slip-knot loop on the hook (though other methods, such as a magic ring or simple folding over of the yarn may be used), pulling another loop through the first loop, and repeating this process to create a chain of a suitable length. The chain is either turned and worked in rows, or joined to the beginning of the row with a slip stitch and worked in rounds. Rounds can also be created by working many stitches into a single loop. Stitches are made by pulling one or more loops through each loop of the chain. At any one time at the end of a stitch, there is only one loop left on the hook. Tunisian crochet, however, draws all of the loops for an entire row onto a long hook before working them off one at a time. Like knitting, crochet can be worked either flat or in the round.

Types of stitches

There are five main types of basic stitches. 1. Chain Stitch - the most basic of all stitches and used to begin most projects. 2. Slip Stitch - used to join chain stitch to form a ring. 3. Single Crochet Stitch - easiest stitch to master Single Crochet Stitch Tutorial 4. Half Double Crochet Stitch - the 'in-between' stitch Half-Double Crochet Tutorial 5. Double Crochet Stitch - many uses for this unlimited use stitch Double Crochet Stitch Tutorial hile the horizontal distance covered by these basic stitches is the same, they differ in height and thickness.

Crochet Business

Any stitch using yarnovers uses less yarn than single crochet to produce the same amount of fabric.

Cluster stitches, which are in fact multiple stitches worked together, will use the most length.

Standard crochet stitches like sc and dc also produce a thicker fabric, more like knit garter stitch. This is part of why they use more yarn. Slip stitch can produce a fabric much like stockinette that is thinner and therefore uses less yarn.

It is possible to use the same yarn or wool for both crochet and knitting, providing you have the correct size knitting needles or crochet hooks for the yarn you are using. There are some yarn that are only made for crochet, for example DMC make Cebelia No.10 which is a very thin yarn and works well with Amigurumi crochet.

Differences between crochet and knitting

Most crochet uses one hook and works upon one stitch at a time. Crochet may be worked in circular rounds without any specialized tools, as shown here.

Knitting uses two or more straight needles that carry multiple stitches.

Unlike crochet, knitting requires specialized needles to create circular rounds.

Crochet Business

So what should you make? Well there are plenty of items but to give you some ideas, here is a list of some of the current best sellers on ETSY.

Stevie Nicks Mandela Sweater Coat	$399.00
Granny Square Sweater	$250.00
Original trending Art Painting Flowers	$152.00
Crochet Off the Shoulder Sweater	$150.00
Silk Mohair Shaw	$138.00
Wide Brim Fedora	$109.95
Baby Boy Blanket	$105.12
Sunflower Art	$96.00
Crochet Bridal Shaw white	$86.95
Handmade decorative pillows	$77.90
Sunflower Pot Holder	$14.25
Pumkin Crochet Coasters	$4.25

FREE Knitting Patterns!: https://urlzs.com/okPdR

https://www.knitpicks.com/freebies

For more information on running a crochet business use the link below.

Crochet Business Book for Beginners

by Brian Mahoney

https://www.amazon.com/dp/1539606112

CROCHET BUSINESS
Fast Start Web Resource

https://www.createforless.com/

http://www.yarntree.com/

http://www.knitting-warehouse.com/

http://www.accessoriesunlimitedinc.com/

http://www.lovecrochet.com/

http://www.knitpicks.com/

http://www.koniakow.com/

(poland wholesaler/dropshipper)

http://www.yazzii.com

(Austrailia wholesaler/manufacturers)

https://www.aliexpress.com/

http://www.liquidation.com/

How to get Free Money for Small Business Start up

https://www.amazon.com/dp/1951929144   Paperback

https://urlzs.com/ZamJw   AudioBook

Foreclosure Cleaning Business

Foeclosure Cleaning Business Overview

Estimated Yearly Income: $30,000 - $100,000

Startup Costs: $500 - $3,000

Normal fees: $0.11 per square foot

Marketing/Advertising: Organic SEO, YouTube, Google Ads, Flyers, business website, contact Asset Management companies.

Start up Equipment: Janitor cart, mop, bucket, vacuum, dustpan broom, microfibre cloth, rubber gloves, cleaning solutions

Skills needed: Knowledge of how to use cleaning solutions.

Home Based: Can be operated from home.

Part Time: Can be operated part-time.

Franchises Available? Yes

Online Operation? No

Unexpected Costs: Business Insurance

FORECLOSURE CLEANING BUSINESS

The Foreclosure Cleaning Business can be a six figure business. In the book "the millionaire next door" a cleaning business is one of the most common businesses that average people use to reach a seven figure business.

Recently foreclosures have been on the rise. The great recession of 2008 and now the pandemic of 2020 is going to cause a massive increase in the inventory of foreclosures on the real estate market. So while the recent economic down turns have effected many businesses in a negative way, the foreclosure cleaning business will likely see a massive amount of growth.

Even without covid 19 the U.S. Bureau of Labor statistics predicted a seven percent rise in the growth of hiring for the Janitorial Commercial cleaner. Faster than the average of all occupations. Many of the new jobs are expected to be in the industries of administrative and support services and we are already seeing a massive increase in educational services and healthcare.

Janitors and building cleaners held about 2.4 million jobs in 2018. The largest employers of janitors and building cleaners were as follows:

Services to buildings and dwellings	37%
Elementary and secondary schools; state, local, and private	13
Healthcare and social assistance	7
Government	5
Religious, grantmaking, civic, professional, & similar organizations	5

FORECLOSURE CLEANING BUSINESS

What's Needed to Get Started

Cleaning: How To Do It

1. Include step-by-step procedures for precleaning, cleaning during the job, and daily and final cleanings in

project design or specifications.

2. Assign responsibilities to specific workers for cleaning and for maintaining cleaning equipment.

3. Have sufficient cleaning equipment and supplies before beginning work.

4. If contamination is extensive, conduct precleaning of the dwelling unit. Move or cover all furniture

and other objects.

5. Conduct ongoing cleaning during the job, including regular removal of large and small debris and dust.

Decontamination of all tools, equipment, and worker protection gear is required before it leaves containment areas. Electrical equipment should be wiped and high-efficiency particulate air (HEPA) vacuumed,

not wetted down, to minimize electrocution hazards.

6. Schedule sufficient time (usually 30 minutes to an hour) for a complete daily cleaning, starting at the same

time near the end of each workday after lead hazard control activity has ceased.

FORECLOSURE CLEANING BUSINESS

7. For final cleaning, wait at least 1 hour after active lead hazard control activity has ceased to let dust

particles settle.

8. Use a vacuum cleaner equipped with a HEPA exhaust filter. HEPA vacuum all surfaces in the room

(ceilings, walls, trim, and floors). Start with the ceiling and work down, moving toward the entry door.

Completely clean each room before moving on.

9. Wash all surfaces with a lead-specific detergent, high-phosphate detergent, or other suitable cleaning

agent to dislodge any ground-in contamination, then rinse. Change the cleaning solution after every

room is cleaned.

10. Repeat step 8. To meet clearance standards consistently, a HEPA vacuum, wet wash, and HEPA vacuum cycle is recommended. For interim control projects involving dust removal only, the final HEPA vacuuming step is usually not needed (see Chapter 11). Other cleaning methods are acceptable, as long as clearance criteria are met and workers are not overexposed.

FORECLOSURE CLEANING BUSINESS

11. After final cleaning, perform a visual examination to ensure that all surfaces requiring lead hazard control

have been addressed and all visible dust and debris have been removed. Record findings and correct any

incomplete work. This visual examination should be performed by the owner or an owner's representative

who is independent of the lead hazard control contractor.

12. If other construction work will disturb the lead-based paint surfaces, it should be completed at this point.

If those surfaces are disturbed, repeat the final cleaning step after the other construction work has been

completed.

13. Paint or otherwise seal treated surfaces and interior floors.

14. Conduct a clearance examination (see Chapter 15).

15. If clearance is not achieved, repeat the final cleaning

16. Continue clearance testing and repeated cleaning until the dwelling achieves compliance with all clearance standards. As an incentive to conduct ongoing cleaning and a thorough final cleaning, the cost of repeated

cleaning after failing to achieve clearance should be borne by the contractor as a matter of the job specification, not the owner.

FORECLOSURE CLEANING BUSINESS

17. Do not allow residents to enter the work area until cleaning is completed and clearance is established.

18. Cleaning equipment list:

✦ HEPA vacuums.

✦ Detergent.

✦ Waterproof gloves.

✦ Rags.

✦ Sponges.

✦ Mops.

✦ Buckets.

✦ HEPA vacuum attachments (crevice tools, beater bar for cleaning rugs).

✦ 6-mil plastic bags.

✦ Debris containers.

✦ Waste water containers.

✦ Shovels.

✦ Rakes.

✦ Water-misting sprayers.

✦ 6-mil polyethylene sheeting (or equivalent).

FORECLOSURE CLEANING BUSINESS

Finding Foreclosures to Clean

To find foreclosures to clean you can begin with contacting Foreclosure Asset Management companies. Here are some of the top Foreclosure Asset Management companies.

Asset Management & REO companies

https://www.altisource.com/   (770) 612-7007

https://www.cwcapital.com/   202.715.9500

Green River Capital	(801) 487-3800
Atlas REO	(858) 259-8758
Freddie Mac Homesteps	(800) 972-7555
Equator	(310) 469-9167
Res.NET	(800) 760-7036
Goodman Dean	(800) 930-8999
American Homeowner Preservation	(800) 555-1055
Asset Valuation and Marketing, Inc.	(970) 245-7350
Benjamin Management Group	(310) 640-7771
BPO Direct (Freddie Mac) & FNMA	(202) 752-7000

FORECLOSURE CLEANING BUSINESS

Brighton Real Estate/Pyramid		(801) 456-1703

Broker Price Opinion			(303) 991-9919

Dakota Asset Services			(832) 772-3700

Elam REO Services Co.			(877) 510-7871

Fannie Mae				(202) 752-7000

(Federal National Mortgage Association)

Financial Asset Services, Inc.		(949) 862-1430

First American Title			(866) 575-8484

First Preston				(800) 934-3009

Five Brothers Mortgage Company	(586) 772-7600

A few steps to take to have a successful business:

* Write down a business plan.

* Select the best equipment suppliers for your needs.

* Model after other successful businesses.

* Get business insurance and proper permits/licenses.

* Take Massive Action.

Cleaning Business Entreprenuer by Brian Mahoney

https://www.amazon.com/dp/1537393057

FORECLOSURE CLEANING BUSINESS
WEB RESOURCE GUIDE

Cleaning supplies...

http://www.wholesalejanitorialsupply.com/

http://dollardays.com/wholesale-cleaning-supplies.html

http://www.janitorialsupplies4less.com/

http://www.cleanitsupply.com/

http://www.monsterjanitorial.com

http://www.chem-tex.com/

http://www.discount-carpet-cleaning-machines.com/

http://www.cws-direct.com/

http://www.discountcleaningproducts.com/carpet-extractors-s/1.htm

http://www.cleaning-equipment.com/

http://www.carpet-cleaning-equipment.net/

http://www.aliexpress.com/wholesale/wholesale-carpet-cleaner-equipment.html

How to get Free Money for Small Business Start up

https://www.amazon.com/dp/1951929144   Paperback

https://urlzs.com/ZamJw   AudioBook

Gift Basket Business

GIFT BASKET BUSINESS OVERVIEW

Start-up cost: $500 - $10,000

Potential earnings: $25,000 - $50,000

Normal fees: Baskets are individually priced depending on the contents usually $35-$100 per basket; tailor-made baskets could be priced as high as $350 each.

Marketing/Advertising: Zero Cost Online Marketing. Local newspapers, fliers, bulletin boards, direct mail to busy executives, , online classifieds, website.

Skill set: Natural creativity

Equipment needed: Baskets, filer, and gift materials, glue gun, shrink wrap machine , tables/counters for assembly, vehicle.

Home business potential: Yes

Staff required: No, but it might be a good idea during the holiday seasons of Christmas, Easter and Valentine's Day

Hidden Costs: Shipping costs/vehicle expenses; you may need a liquor license if your baskets contain wine or champagne

GIFT BASKET BUSINESS

Gift baskets make it easy to match a gift to a person's taste. That is what makes the gift basket business so amazing.

Finding the "perfect gift" for a special occasion is, for many people, can be very difficult. Running around from store to store only to find high priced or bad quality items can make gift giving very frustrating. When it comes to gift giving it's always a good idea to put some thought into the gift and match a good gift for the person.

Gift-giving isn't just a seasonal obligation. -- There's always a holiday on the horizon. Many people are becoming more proactive by creating affordable, unique gift ideas. These gift givers have discovered the exciting business of custom-made and often Gourmet Gift Baskets.

GIFT BASKETS

A gift basket, or fruit basket is typically a gift delivered to the recipient at their home or workplace. A variety of gift baskets exist: some contain fruit; while others might contain dry or canned foods such as tea, crackers and jam; or the basket might include a combination of fruit and dried good items. Gourmet gift baskets typically include exotic fruit, and often include quality cheese and wine, as well as other nonfood items.

GIFT BASKET BUSINESS

FRUIT BOUQUET

A fruit bouquet is a fruit arrangement in the form of bouquet. The fruit is cut in the shape of flowers and leaves, and is arranged in the container with the help of sticks. A complete arrangement looks like a bouquet of flowers. Typically, a fruit bouquet is delivered to the recipient at their home or workplace.

Often these bouquets will be made to suit the recipients' needs, such as diabetic, vegan, vegetarian, gluten intolerance or wheat intolerance. Common fruit bouquet items include apples, artichokes, avocados, bananas, cheeses, grapes, lychees, mangoes, oranges, papayas, pineapples, pomegranates, strawberries, and Chocolates.

Often a gift basket will have a theme, such as for an occasion, like Christmas, Easter, Mother's Day, Father's Day, Thanksgiving, graduation, birthday, anniversary, baby shower, housewarming, or Valentine's Day. One can also send a sympathy gift basket or get well gift basket. A basket can be made to suit the dietary restrictions of the recipient, such as diabetic, peanut allergy, vegan, vegetarian, gluten or wheat intolerance.,

GIFT BASKET BUSINESS

Corporate Gift Baskets

Many Corporate entities such as law firms, accounting, insurance, financing and banking, Medical and Pharmaceutical industries send higher end gift baskets for important clients to say 'thank you' for your business. Gifting is an important gesture in showing appreciation and confidence.

Baby Gift Baskets

The addition of a new member to a family is both an exciting and challenging time. Many people feel that sending a gift basket is the best way to express ones excitement and congratulations on the new little bundle of joy. Common items found in baby gift baskets include onesies, teethers, sleepers, rattles, plush stuffies, socks, wash cloths – all things the new parents will find very useful as they adjust to life with their new baby.

Wine Gift Baskets

There are plenty of wine lovers out there. That's why wine gift baskets can make the perfect gift. But creating them can be expensive. So below you have a list composed by Forbes Magazine of the top 19 great tasting wines that you can purchase for about twenty dollars!

1. Filipa Pato Rosé 'Metodo Tradicional' sparkling wine, Bairrada, Portugal, $15.

GIFT BASKET BUSINESS

2. 2012 Domaine Wachau, Riesling Federspiel Terrassen, Austria $18

3. 2011 Garbó Negre, Spain, $19.

4. 2012 Campo Viejo Garnacha Rioja, Spain, $19.

5. 2011 La Quercia Montepulciano d'Abruzzo, Italy, $12.

6. 2008 La Valentina Spelt, Italy, $20.

7, 2012 Sofia Chardonnay, Monterey, CA, $19.

8. 2005 Beronia Reserva Rioja, Spain $20.

9. 2011 Thomas Goss Cabernet Sauvignon, Australia, $17.

10. 2012 Maison Joseph Drouhin Laforet Bourgogne Chardonnay, France, $18.

11. 2011 Inama 'Vin Soave' Soave Classico, Italy, $15.

12. 2012 Hogwash Rosé, CA, $15.99.

13. 2012 Terras Gauda Abadia de San Campio, Albarino, Rias Biaxas, Spain, $20.

14. 2009 Altolandon Rayuelo, Spain, $20.

15. 2010 Sobon Estate Zinfandel, Amador, CA, $17.

GIFT BASKET BUSINESS

16. 2012 Santa Carolina Sauvignon Blanc, Chile, $12.99.

17. 2010 Ouled Thaleb Syrah, Morocco, $16.

18. 2012 Apaltagua Rosé of Carmenere, Central Valley, Chile, $12.

19. 2012 Allan Scott Pinot Noir, Marlborough, New Zealand, $14.99.

After you purchase your wine, you can add cheese and other tasty treats to your gift basket. You can add cheese bars, wedges of cheese, cheese spreads, chips, meat sticks or slim Jims, crackers, gourmet mustards, pretzels, hersheys dark chocolate, a cheese board and cheese knife.

Candy Gift Baskets

Candy gift baskets can offer the perfect sweet tooth cure for your family, friends and business associates. Here are some ideas for candy gift baskets.

GIFT BASKET BUSINESS

Healthy Candy Ideas

1. Sugar-free candy bars: Hershey now has an entire line of sugar free candy bars that retail for about $3.00 a bag.

2. Flavanol-rich chocolate: Mars is coming out with a product that is high in flavanol, which is a type of anti-oxidant.

3. Fruit juice concentrate candies: Instructables has fruit juice gummy candies.

4. Diet candy: Many large makers are now offering a whole line of healthier candy which they are labeling as diet candy.

5. Apples, oranges and other fresh fruits: And, it never hurts to add to your candy gift basket a few pieces of whole fresh fruits such as apples, orange and raisins.

GIFT BASKET BUSINESS

TOP SELLING CANDY IDEAS

According to Jane Wells a reporter for CNBC here is the top 5 candies in the world. The nice thing about this list is that the candies are easy to fine and are sold almost everywhere.

5. KitKat Bar

4. Hershey Bar

3. Snickers

2. M&Ms

1. Reese's

For more information on a Gift Basket Business:

https://www.amazon.com/dp/B01KJYEHV4

WEB RESOURCE GUIDE GIFT BASKETS SUPPLIES

1. http://goo.gl/lvSY8G

2. http://www.giftbasketwholesalesupply.com/

3. http://www.giftbasketsupplies.com/Index.aspx?key=cat

4. http://www.americabasket.com/supplies.html

5. https://www.nashvillewraps.com/

6. http://www.giftbasketdropshipping.com/

7. http://www.buhiimports.com/index.html

8. http://www.dutchvalleyfoods.com/

9. http://www.naturesgardencandles.com/

10. http://www.ediblenature.com/

11. http://www.discountbeautycenter.com/

12. http://www.esutras.com/

How to get Free Money for Small Business Start up

https://www.amazon.com/dp/1951929144   Paperback

https://urlzs.com/ZamJw   AudioBook

JEWELRY BUSINESS

JEWELRY BUSINESS OVERVIEW

JEWELRY BUSINESS

Estimated Yearly Income: $25,000 - $70,000

Startup Costs: $100 - $1,000

Normal fees: $10 - $59,160.74 per piece (Etsy)

Marketing/Advertising: Etsy.com, eBay.com, Organic SEO, YouTube, Google Ads, Flyers, art studios, art supply stores, trade and craft shows, business website

Start up Equipment: jeweler loop, magnifying glass, melting equipment, molds, pliers, vices,

Skills needed: Creativity, GIA certificate (Gemological Institute of America) not required, helpful.

Home Based: Can be operated from home.

Part Time: Can be operated part-time.

Franchises Available? No

Online Business Potential: Yes

Hidden Cost: Business Insurance

JEWELRY BUSINESS

Jewellery design is the art or profession of designing and creating jewellery. This is one of civilization's earliest forms of decoration, dating back at least 7,000 years to the oldest known human societies in Mesopotamia and Egypt. The art has taken many forms throughout the centuries, from the simple beadwork of ancient times to the sophisticated metalworking and gem cutting known in the modern day.

Before an article of jewellery is created, design concepts are rendered followed by detailed technical drawings generated by a jewellery designer, a professional who is trained in the architectural and functional knowledge of materials, fabrication techniques, composition, wearability and market trends.

Traditional hand-drawing and drafting methods are still utilized in designing jewellery, particularly at the conceptual stage. However, a shift is taking place to computer-aided design programs like Rhinoceros 3D and Matrix. Whereas the traditionally hand-illustrated jewel is typically translated into wax or metal directly by a skilled craftsman, a CAD model is generally used as the basis for a CNC cut or 3D printed 'wax' pattern to be used in the rubber molding or lost wax casting processes.

JEWELRY BUSINESS

Once conceptual/ideation is complete, the design is rendered and fabricated using the necessary materials for proper adaptation to the function of the object. For example, 24K gold was used in ancient jewellery design because it was more accessible than silver as source material. Before the 1st century many civilizations also incorporated beads into jewellery. Once the discovery of gemstones and gem cutting became more readily available, the art of jewellery ornamentation and design shifted. The earliest documented gemstone cut was done by Theophilus Presbyter (c. 1070–1125), who practiced and developed many applied arts and was a known goldsmith. Later, during the 14th century, medieval lapidary technology evolved to include cabochons and cameos.

Early jewellery design commissions were often constituted by nobility or the church to honor an event or as wearable ornamentation. Within the structure of early methods, enameling and repoussé became standard methods for creating ornamental wares to demonstrate wealth, position, or power. These early techniques created a specific complex design element that later would forge the Baroque movement in jewellery design.

Traditionally, jewels were seen as sacred and precious; however, beginning in the 1900s, jewellery has started to be objectified. Additionally, no one trend can be seen as the history of jewellery design for this time period.

JEWELRY BUSINESS

The largest employers of craft and Jewelry artists were as follows:

Self-employed workers   55%

Independent artists, writers, and performers   9

Federal government, excluding postal service   7

Motion picture and sound recording industries   3

Personal care services   2

Work Environment

Many artists work in fine- or commercial-art studios located in office buildings, warehouses, or lofts. Others work in private studios in their homes. Some artists share studio space, where they also may exhibit their work.

Studios are usually well lit and ventilated. However, artists may be exposed to fumes from glue, paint, ink, and other materials. They may also have to deal with dust or other residue from filings, splattered paint, or spilled cleaning and other fluids. Artists often wear protective gear, such as breathing masks and goggles, in order to remain safe from exposure to harmful materials. Ceramic and glass artists must use caution in working with materials that may break into sharp pieces and in using equipment that can get very hot, such as kilns.

JEWELRY BUSINESS

Work Schedules

Most craft and Jewelry artists work full time, although part-time and variable schedules are also common. Many hold another job in addition to their work as an artist. During busy periods, artists may work additional hours to meet deadlines. Those who are self-employed usually determine their own schedules.

How to Become a Craft or Jewelry Artist

Craft and Jewelry artists

Education gives artists an opportunity to develop their portfolio, which is a collection of an artist's work that demonstrates his or her styles and abilities.

Craft and Jewelry artists improve their skills through practice and repetition. A bachelor's degree is the common for these artists.

Education

Most Jewelry artists pursue postsecondary education to improve their skills and job prospects. A formal educational credential is typically not needed to be a craft artist. However, it is difficult to gain adequate artistic skills without some formal education. For example, high school art classes can teach prospective craft artists the basic drawing skills they need.

JEWELRY BUSINESS

A number of colleges and universities offer bachelor's and master's degrees in subjects related to fine arts. In addition to studio art and art history, postsecondary programs may include core subjects, such as English, marketing, social science, and natural science. Independent schools of art and design also offer postsecondary education programs, which can lead to a certificate in an art-related specialty or to an associate's, bachelor's, or master's degree in fine arts.

The National Association of Schools of Art and Design (NASAD) accredits more than 360 postsecondary institutions with programs in art and design. Most of these schools award a degree in art.

Medical illustrators must have artistic ability and a detailed knowledge of human or animal anatomy, living organisms, and surgical and medical procedures. They usually need a bachelor's degree that combines art and premedical courses. Medical illustrators may choose to get a master's degree in medical illustration. Four accredited schools offer this degree in the United States.

Education gives artists an opportunity to develop their portfolio, which is a collection of an artist's work that demonstrates his or her styles and abilities. Portfolios are essential, because art directors, clients, and others look at them when deciding whether to hire an artist or to buy the artist's work. In addition to compiling a physical portfolio, many artists choose to create a portfolio online.

JEWELRY BUSINESS

Those who want to teach fine arts at public elementary or secondary schools usually must have a teaching certificate in addition to a bachelor's degree. For more information on workers who teach art classes, see the profiles on kindergarten and elementary school teachers, middle school teachers, high school teachers, career and technical education teachers, and postsecondary teachers.

Training

Craft and Jewelry artists improve their skills through practice and repetition. They can train in several ways other than, or in addition to, formal schooling. Craft and Jewelry artists may train with simpler projects before attempting something more ambitious.

Some artists learn on the job from more experienced artists. Others attend noncredit classes or workshops or take private lessons, which may be offered in artists' studios or at community colleges, art centers, galleries, museums, or other art-related institutions.

Important Qualities

Artistic ability. Craft and Jewelry artists create artwork and other objects that are visually appealing or thought provoking. This endeavor usually requires significant skill and attention to detail in one or more art forms.

JEWELRY BUSINESS

Business skills. Craft and Jewelry artists must promote themselves and their art to build a reputation and to sell their art. They often study the market for their crafts or artwork to increase their understanding of what prospective customers might want. Craft and Jewelry artists also may sell their work on the internet, so developing an online presence is often an important part of their art sales.

Creativity. Artists must have active imaginations to develop new and original ideas for their work.

Customer-service skills. Craft and Jewelry artists, especially those who sell their work themselves, must be good at dealing with customers and prospective buyers.

Dexterity. Artists must be good at manipulating tools and materials to create their art.

Interpersonal skills. Artists should be comfortable interacting with people, including customers, gallery owners, and the public.

Self-employed and **freelance artists** try to establish a set of clients who regularly contract for work. Some of these artists are recognized for their skill in a specialty, such as cartooning or illustrating children's books. They may earn enough to choose the types of projects they undertake.

For more information on how to set up a freelance business:

Secrets to Making Money Now with Freelance Jobs Online by Brian Mahoney

https://www.amazon.com/dp/1981365931

JEWELRY WEB RESOURCE GUIDE

Jewelry Business Web Sites

http://www.supplyjewelry.com/

http://www.bodycandy.com/

https://silver-jewelry-planet.com/

http://wholesalejewelryzone.com/

http://www.wholesaleperuvianjewelry.com/

http://www.cerijewelry.com/

http://www.sunjewelry.com/

http://www.wholesalejewelrysupply.com/en/

How to get Free Money for Small Business Start up

https://www.amazon.com/dp/1951929144   Paperback

https://urlzs.com/ZamJw   AudioBook

How to Make Jewelry Video Tutorial

https://urlzs.com/d5sKH

Lawn Care Business

LAWN CARE BUSINESS OVERVIEW

LAWN CARE BUSINESS

Estimated Yearly Income: $25,000-$50,000

Startup Costs: $200-$1,500

Normal fees: $15-$20 per hour or flat rate of $50-$100 per job.

Marketing/Advertising: Organic SEO, YouTube, Google Ads, Flyers on front doors, Zero Cost Online Marketing, Internet Marketing, Business Cards, Classified Ads, Yellow Pages, Online Yellow Pages, Referrals, Direct Mail Postcards, Business Groups, business website

Start up Equipment: Power mower, rakes, leaf blower, power trimmer and spreader, pickup truck or station wagon

Skills needed: Lawn care knowledge, stamina

Home Based: Can be operated from home.

Part Time: Can be operated part-time.

Hidden Costs:

Insurance & licensing; Travel Expenses, Equipment rental

LAWN CARE BUSINESS

What Lawn Care Workers Do

Lawn Care workers

Lawn Care workers ensure that the grounds of houses, businesses, parks, and urban infrastructure are attractive, orderly, and healthy in order to provide a pleasant outdoor environment.

Duties

Lawn Care workers typically do the following:

- Mow, edge, and fertilize lawns
- Weed and mulch landscape beds
- Trim hedges, shrubs, and small trees
- Remove dead, damaged, or unwanted trees
- Plant flowers, trees, and shrubs
- Water lawns, landscapes, and gardens
- Monitor and maintain plant health

Lawn Care workers are generally under the direction of a professional grounds manager and perform a variety of tasks to achieve a pleasant and functional outdoor environment. They also care for indoor gardens and plants in commercial and public facilities, such as malls, hotels, and botanical gardens.

LAWN CARE BUSINESS

The following are examples of types of Lawn Care workers:

Landscaping workers plant trees, flowers, and shrubs to create new outdoor spaces or upgrade existing ones. They also trim, fertilize, mulch, and water plants. Some grade and install lawns or construct hardscapes such as walkways, patios, and decks. Others help install lighting or sprinkler systems. Landscaping workers are employed in a variety of residential and commercial settings, such as homes, apartment buildings, office buildings, shopping malls, and hotels and motels.

Groundskeeping workers, also called groundskeepers, maintain grounds. They care for plants and trees, rake and mulch leaves, and clear snow from walkways. They work on athletic fields, golf courses, cemeteries, university campuses, and parks, as well as in many of the same settings that landscaping workers work. They also see to the proper upkeep of sidewalks, parking lots, fountains, fences, planters, and benches, as well as groundskeeping equipment.

Groundskeeping workers who care for athletic fields keep natural and artificial turf in top condition, mark out boundaries, and paint turf with team logos and names before events. They mow, water, fertilize, and aerate the fields regularly. They must ensure that the underlying soil on fields with natural turf has the composition required to allow proper drainage and to support the grass used on the field. In sports venues, they vacuum and disinfect synthetic turf to prevent the growth of harmful bacteria and they remove the turf and replace the cushioning pad periodically.

LAWN CARE BUSINESS

Tree trimmers and pruners, also called arborists, cut away dead or excess branches from trees or shrubs to clear utility lines, roads, and sidewalks. Many of these workers strive to improve the appearance and health of trees and plants, and some specialize in diagnosing and treating tree diseases. Others specialize in pruning, trimming, and shaping ornamental trees and shrubs. Tree trimmers and pruners use chain saws, chippers, and stump grinders while on the job. When trimming near power lines, they usually work on truck-mounted lifts and use power pruners.

How to Become a Lawn Care Worker

Some workers obtain a degree in landscape design or horticulture.

Most Lawn Care workers need no formal education and are trained on the job. Most states require licensing for workers who apply pesticides and fertilizers.

Education

Although most Lawn Care jobs have no education requirements, some employers may require formal education or certification in areas such as landscape design, horticulture, or arboriculture.

Licenses, Certifications, and Registrations

LAWN CARE BUSINESS

Most states require workers who apply pesticides and fertilizers to be licensed. Obtaining a license usually involves passing a test on the proper use and disposal of insecticides, herbicides, and fungicides.

Although professional certification is not required, it can demonstrate competency and reliability for prospective clients and employers.

The National Association of Landscape Professionals offers seven certifications in landscaping and Lawn Care for workers at various experience levels.

The Tree Care Industry Association offers certification for tree care safety professionals.

The International Society of Arboriculture offers six certifications for workers at various experience levels.

The Professional Grounds Management Society offers certification for workers at various experience levels.

Training

LAWN CARE BUSINESS

A short period of on-the-job training is usually enough to teach new hires the skills they need, which often include how to plant and maintain areas and how to use mowers, trimmers, leaf blowers, small tractors, and other equipment. Large institutional employers such as golf courses, university campuses, or municipalities may supplement on-the-job training with coursework in horticulture, arboriculture, urban forestry, insect and disease diagnosis, tree climbing, or small-engine repair.

Important Qualities

Physical stamina. Lawn Care workers must be capable of doing physically strenuous labor for long hours, occasionally in extreme heat or cold.

Self-motivated. Because they often work with little supervision, Lawn Care workers must be able to do their job independently.

Visualization. Lawn Care workers must have the ability to imagine how plants, trees, shrubs, and other landscaping will look before planting or trimming.

LAWN CARE BUSINESS

Pay

The median hourly wage for Lawn Care workers was $14.85 in May 2019. The median wage is the wage at which half the workers in an occupation earned more than that amount and half earned less. The lowest 10 percent earned less than $10.53, and the highest 10 percent earned more than $23.18.

Median hourly wages for Lawn Care workers in May 2019 were as follows:

Tree trimmers and pruners $19.22

Pesticide handlers, sprayers,

and applicators, vegetation   17.23

Lawn Care workers, all other   15.43

Landscaping and groundskeeping workers   14.63

In May 2019, the median hourly wages for Lawn Care workers in the top industries in which they worked were as follows:

LAWN CARE BUSINESS

Educational services; state, local, and private $16.39

Government 15.10

Services to buildings and dwellings 15.09

Amusement, gambling, and recreation industries 12.84

Many Lawn Care jobs are seasonal. Jobs are most common in the spring, summer, and fall, when planting, mowing, and trimming are most frequent. However, many also provide other seasonal services, such as snow removal and installation and removal of holiday décor.

LAWN CARE Wholesale Web Rolodex

Lawn Care Equipment

http://www.equipmenttraderonline.com/

http://www.libertydiscount.com/

http://www.wholesaledistributorsnet.com/garden.html

https://gsaauctions.gov/gsaauctions/gsaauctions/

http://www.lawncareequipmentco.com/

http://www.liquidation.com/general-merchandise/wholesale-lawn.html

https://www.alibaba.com/showroom/lawn-mowers-wholesale.html

http://www.powerequipmentdirect.com/

http://www.lawnsite.com/

How to get Free Money for Small Business Start up

https://www.amazon.com/dp/1951929144   Paperback

https://urlzs.com/ZamJw   AudioBook

Locksmith Business

LOCKSMITH BUSINESS OVERVIEW

Start-up Cost:

$5,000 - $10,000

Potential Earnings:

$20,000 - $35,000

Typical Fees:

$2-$4 for a standard key, $50-$175 vechicle keys with an electronic or transponder chip, $40 - $100 minimum fee plus labor charges of $20 - $30 per lock to replace home door locks

Marketing/Advertising: Organic SEO, YouTube, Google Ads, Flyers on front doors, Zero Cost Online Marketing, Internet Marketing, Business Cards, Classified Ads, Yellow Pages, Online Yellow Pages,Referrals, Direct Mail Postcards, Business Groups, business website

Qualifications:

Mechanical aptitude, training (correspondence course)

Equipment needed:

Key cutting machine, lock picking implements, product stock/supply, vehicle

Staff Required: No

Hidden Costs:

Equipment maintenance costs, insurance, vehicle expenses

LOCKSMITH BUSINESS

Locksmithing is the science and art of making and defeating locks. Locksmithing is a traditional trade and in most countries requires completion of an apprenticeship. The level of formal education required varies from country to country, from a simple training certificate awarded by an employer, to a full diploma from an engineering college (such as in Australia) in addition to time spent working as an apprentice.

Work

Locks have been constructed for over 2500 years, initially out of wood and later out of metal. Historically, locksmiths would make the entire lock, working for hours hand cutting screws and doing much file-work. Lock designs became significantly more complicated in the 18th century, and locksmiths often specialised in repairing or designing locks. After the rise of cheap mass production, the vast majority of locks are repaired by swapping of parts or like-for-like replacement or upgraded to modern mass-production items. Until more recently, safes and strongboxes were the exceptions to this, and to this day large vaults are custom designed and built at great cost, as the cost of this is lower than the very limited scope for mass production would allow, and the risk of a copy being obtained and defeated as practice is removed.

LOCKSMITH BUSINESS

Although fitting of keys to replace lost keys to automobiles and homes and the changing of keys for homes and businesses to maintain security are still an important part of locksmithing, locksmiths today are primarily involved in the installation of higher quality locksets and the design, implementation and management of keying and key control systems. Most locksmiths also do electronic lock servicing, such as making keys for transponder-equipped vehicles and the implementation and application of access control systems protecting individuals and assets for many large institutions.

In terms of physical security, a locksmith's work frequently involves making a determination of the level of risk to an individual or institution and then recommending and implementing appropriate combinations of equipment and policies to create "security layers" which exceed the reasonable gain to an intruder or attacker. The more different security layers are implemented, the more the requirement for additional skills and knowledge and tools to defeat them all. But because each layer comes at an expense to the customer, the application of appropriate levels without exceeding reasonable costs to the customer is often very important and requires a skilled and knowledgeable locksmith to determine.

LOCKSMITH BUSINESS

Employment

Locksmiths may be commercial (working out of a storefront), mobile (working out of a vehicle), institutional (employed by an institution) or investigatory (forensic locksmiths) or may specialise in one aspect of the skill, such as an automotive lock specialist, a master key system specialist or a safe technician. Many are also security consultants, but not every security consultant has the skills and knowledge of a locksmith. Locksmiths are frequently certified in specific skill areas or to a level of skill within the trade. This is separate from certificates of completion of training courses. In determining skill levels, certifications from manufacturers or locksmith associations are usually more valid criteria than certificates of completion. Some locksmiths decide to call themselves "Master Locksmiths" whether they are fully trained or not, and some training certificates appear quite authoritative.

The majority of locksmiths also work on any existing door hardware, not just locking mechanisms. This includes door closer's, door hinges, electric strikes, frame repairs and other door hardware.

LOCKSMITH BUSINESS

Online Locksmithing Schools

Ashworth College

The Locksmithing program provides students with a basic understanding of the materials, tools and processes used by locksmith professionals to install modern security hardware in homes, businesses and automobiles.

This program also provides students the opportunity to validate their locksmithing proficiency by successfully completing the Fundamentals Locksmith exam, offered by the Associated Locksmiths of America.

Tuition 2020: $899.00 Monthly Payment : $49.00

Stratford Career Institute

Stratford Career Institute is a privately owned correspondence school established in 1991 that offers at-home vocational training programs to students in North America.

Tuition 2020: $689.00 Monthly Payment : $37.16

Penn Foster Career School

In the Penn Foster Career School Professional Locksmith & Home Security Technician training program you'll learn about duplicating keys, the methods of opening locks without keys, as well as installing door locks, security devices, safes, vaults, and panic hardware.

Tuition 2020: $839.00 Monthly Payment : $55.00

LOCKSMITH BUSINESS

LOCKSMITH TERMS

Bitting - The bitting of a key is the physical arrangement of the bits of the key that engage with the locking mechanism. The bitting instructs a locksmith how to cut a certain key, to replace a lost key or make an additional copy.

Bolt stump - In lever tumbler locks, a bolt stump is a rectangular part located above the talon, and passes through the slot in the levers as the bolt moves.

Break - A break in the pins is a separation in one or more sections of the pin used to encode the lock for a specific key or set of keys in a master keying system.

Dual custody - A dual custody locking system is one where two different keys, generally given to different people, are required to open the lock. These are often used in safe deposit boxes.

Face plate - A metal plate on the lockset itself (on the door, not the jamb) is called a face plate.

False gate - A false gate is a mechanical element on levers in lever tumbler locks or discs in disc tumbler locks to make the lock more difficult to pick.

LOCKSMITH BUSINESS

Glass relocking device -   A glass relocking device is a piece of glass, usually tempered, placed where it might be expected to break in a burglary attack. It is attached, usually with wires, to one or more spring-loaded bolts, which are often randomly located. A drill or torch may break the glass, releasing the bolts.

Lock housing -   The lock housing, also known as the bible[citation needed], refers to the part of the lock that does not move when the lock is opened. The driver pins of a pin-tumbler lock are located in the bible.

Plug -   The plug is the part of a cylinder lock which is designed to turn when a key is inserted.

Plug follower -   A plug follower is a device used in the assembly and disassembly of locks; it is a solid cylinder that is used to push the plug out of the lock, while preventing the springs and driver pins from moving.

Relocking device -   A relocking device (RLD) (a.k.a. "external relocker") is an auxiliary locking device intended to be activated during an attempted burglary of a safe or vault. Such a device will keep a safe or vault locked even if the primary lock is defeated. This independent mechanism is designed to maintain the locked state of a safe even if the lock itself is destroyed. This auxiliary locking device usually consists of a spring-loaded bolt of some type, held in check by a bracket or cable that is rigged to release the mechanism in a burglary attempt. The device will either block the main boltwork from retracting or block the door from opening.

LOCKSMITH BUSINESS

Glass relockers are one of the most common types of relockers used in today's safes. Relockers are typically designed for one-time activation, meaning that once they are triggered the device is locked "permanently" and can only be opened by brute force.

Security pin -   A security pin is a pin designed in a non-standard way to attempt to prevent the lock from being picked. Examples of security pins include serrated pins, spools, and mushroom pins.

Shear line -   In a cylinder lock, the shear line (also known as the split line in Australia), is where the inner cylinder ends and the outer cylinder begins. When a break in the pin is reached by picking, the pin will "hang" at the shearline due to the space between the inner and outer cylinder. This "imperfection" in the lock mechanism is an unavoidable defect in the manufacturing process that allows for lock picking.

Snib -   A snib is a device to engage or disengage a lock without the use of a key. In Scottish English or Irish English, the word is sometimes used as a synonym for lock.

Spool pin -   A spool pin is a type of security pin used to prevent picking in a pin tumbler lock. The pin is shaped like a cable reel.

LOCKSMITH BUSINESS

Strike plate - A strike plate is a metal plate affixed to a doorjamb with a hole or holes for the bolt of the door. When the door is closed, the bolt extends into the hole in the strike plate and holds the door closed. The strike plate protects the jamb against friction from the bolt and increases security in the case of a jamb made of a softer material (such as wood) than the strike plate. Some strike plates have their hole size and placement calculated so a spring-bolt extends into the hole, but an adjacent anti-retraction device remains depressed, preventing the bolt from being retracted unless the lock is turned.

Talon - The part of the bolt of a lock upon which the key presses as it is turned.

Thermal relocking device - Designed as a defense against torch attacks, these are simply relocking devices equipped with a fusible link designed to melt and release the relocking device if the temperature inside the door exceeds a certain temperature (usually 65 °C), as would happen in a torch attack.

For more information on running a Locksmith Business:

How to Start a Locks and Locksmithing Business, The Best of Locksmith Books: Start with Crowd Funding, Get Grants & Get the Right Locksmithing Tools & Locksmith Training

https://www.amazon.com/dp/1979881723

Locksmith Web Wholesale Resource Rolodex

Key Cutting Machine

https://www.keyprom8.com/

http://www.lockpicks.com/

https://urlzs.com/CdbDE

Supplies automotive

http://www.transponderisland.com/

Supplies

http://mysecuritypro.com/

http://www.anthonylockandsafe.com/

http://www.911locksmith.com/index.php

Tools

http://www.lockpicks.com/

https://www.aliexpress.com/popular/locksmith-tools-sale.html

How to get Free Money for Small Business Start up

https://www.amazon.com/dp/1951929144   Paperback

https://urlzs.com/ZamJw   AudioBook

Animal Care & Pet Sitting Business

Animal Care & Pet Sitting Business Overview

Start-up Cost: $150-$200
Potential Earnings: $10,000-$25,00

Typical Fees: $20-$40 per day for one pet $10 for each additional pet. $75-$85 overnight. Additional for walking, house training for puppies, holidays or special medical care.

Advertising:

Word of mouth, Flyers in Vets office & Pet supply stores, Zero Cost Online Marketing, Internet Marketing, Business Cards, Classified Ads, Yellow Pages, Online Yellow Pages, Website, Referrals, Direct Mail Postcards, Business Groups

Qualifications:

Love of Animals, Animal 1st Aid, Organization skills

Equipment Needed:

Vehicle, Pet sitting software, Phone, computer, fax/printer, e-mail, hammer and nails for posting signs.

Home Business Potential: Yes

Staff Required: No (yes for a backup)

Hidden Costs:

Insurance & licensing; Travel Expenses, Trip to Vet

Animal Care & Pet Sitting

What Animal Care and Pet Sitters Do

Animal care and Pet Sitters attend to animals. They feed, groom, bathe, and exercise pets and other nonfarm animals.

Animal care and Pet Sitters typically do the following:

Give food and water to animals

Clean equipment and the living spaces of animals

Monitor animals and record details of their diet, physical condition, and behavior

Examine animals for signs of illness or injury

Exercise animals

Bathe animals, trim nails, clip hair, and attend to other grooming needs

Train animals to obey or to behave in a specific manner

The following are types of animal care and Pet Sitters :

Animal trainers teach animals a variety of skills, such as obedience, performance, riding, security, and assisting people with disabilities. They familiarize animals with human voices and contact, and they teach animals to respond to commands. Most animal trainers work with dogs and horses, but some work with marine mammals, such as dolphins. Trainers teach a variety of skills. For example, some train dogs to guide people with disabilities, or they may train animals for a competition.

Animal Care & Pet Sitting

Groomers specialize in maintaining a pet's appearance. They typically groom dogs and cats, which may include cutting, trimming, shampooing, and styling fur; clipping nails; and cleaning ears. Groomers also schedule appointments, sell products to pet owners, and identify problems that may require veterinary attention.

Groomers may work in or operate a grooming salon, kennel, veterinary clinic, pet supply store, or mobile grooming service, a self-contained business that travels to clients' homes.

Grooms work at stables, caring for horses and maintaining equipment. Responsibilities include feeding, grooming, and exercising horses; cleaning stalls; polishing saddles; and organizing the tack room, which stores harnesses, saddles, and bridles. Experienced grooms sometimes help train horses.

Kennel attendants care for pets, often overnight, in place of owners. They clean cages and dog runs and feed, exercise, and play with animals. Experienced attendants also may provide basic healthcare, bathe animals, and attend to other basic grooming needs.

Nonfarm animal caretakers typically work with cats and dogs in animal shelters or rescue leagues. All caretakers attend to the basic needs of animals and may have administrative duties, such as keeping records, answering questions from the public, educating visitors about pet health, and screening people who want to adopt an animal. Experienced caretakers may have more responsibilities, such as helping to vaccinate or euthanize animals alongside a veterinarian.

Animal Care & Pet Sitting

Pet sitters look after animals while the pet owner is away. Most pet sitters feed, walk, and play with pets daily. They go to the pet owner's home, allowing the pet to stay in its familiar surroundings and follow its routine. Experienced pet sitters also may bathe, groom, or train pets. Pet sitters typically watch over dogs, but some also take care of cats and other pets.

Zookeepers care for animals in zoos. They plan diets, feed animals, and monitor the animals' eating patterns. They also clean the animals' enclosures and monitor behavior for signs of illness or injury. Depending on the size of the zoo, they may work with one species or multiple species of animals. Zookeepers may help raise young animals, and they often spend time answering questions from the public.

How to Become an Animal Care & Pet Sitter

Animal care and Pet Sitters

Most animal care and Pet Sitters have a high school diploma and learn the occupation on the job.

Animal care and Pet Sitters typically have a high school diploma or equivalent and learn the occupation on the job. Many employers prefer to hire people who have experience with animals.

Education

Animal care and Pet Sitters typically need at least a high school diploma or equivalent.

Animal Care & Pet Sitting

Although pet groomers typically learn by working under the guidance of an experienced groomer, they can also attend grooming schools.

Animal trainers usually need a high school diploma or equivalent, although some positions may require a bachelor's degree. For example, marine mammal trainers usually need a bachelor's degree in marine biology, animal science, biology, or a related field.

Dog trainers and horse trainers may take courses at community colleges or vocational and private training schools.

Most zoos require zookeepers to have a bachelor's degree in biology, animal science, or a related field.

Training

Most animal care and Pet Sitters learn through on-the-job training.

Animal trainers may learn their skills from an experienced trainer. Pet groomers often learn their trade under the guidance of an experienced groomer.

Licenses, Certifications, and Registrations

Although not required, certifications may help workers establish their credentials and enhance their skills. For example, professional associations and private vocational and state-approved trade schools offer certification for dog trainers.

Animal Care & Pet Sitting

The National Dog Groomers Association of America offers certification for master status as a groomer. Both the National Association of Professional Pet Sitters and Pet Sitters International offer a home-study certification program for pet sitters. Marine mammal trainers should be certified in scuba diving.

Many states require self-employed animal care and Pet Sitters to have a business license.

Other Experience

For many animal care and Pet Sitters positions, it helps to have experience working with animals. Volunteering and internships at zoos and aquariums are excellent ways to gain such experience.

Important Qualities

Compassion. Animal care and Pet Sitters must be compassionate when dealing with animals and their owners. They should treat animals with kindness.

Customer-service skills. Animal care and Pet Sitters should understand pet owners' needs so they can provide excellent customer service. Some workers may need to deal with distraught pet owners. For example, caretakers working in animal shelters may need to reassure owners looking for a lost pet.

Detail oriented. Animal care and Pet Sitters are often responsible for maintaining records and monitoring changes in animals' behavior.

Animal Care & Pet Sitting

Patience. All animal caretakers and animal trainers need to be patient when working with animals.

Physical stamina. Animal care and Pet Sitters must be able to kneel, crawl, and lift heavy supplies, such as bags of food.

Problem-solving skills. Animal trainers must be able to assess whether animals are responding to teaching methods and to identify which methods are successful.

Reliability. Animal care and Pet Sitters need to care for animals on schedule and in a timely manner.

PAY

The median annual wage for animal trainers was $30,430 in May 2019. The median wage is the wage at which half the workers in an occupation earned more than that amount and half earned less. The lowest 10 percent earned less than $20,810, and the highest 10 percent earned more than $59,110.

The median annual wage for nonfarm animal caretakers was $24,780 in May 2019. The lowest 10 percent earned less than $18,630, and the highest 10 percent earned more than $38,630.

In May 2019, the median annual wages for animal trainers in the top industries in which they worked were as follows:

Animal Care & Pet Sitting

Arts, entertainment, and recreation $33,910

Retail trade   24,730

In May 2019, the median annual wages for nonfarm animal caretakers in the top industries in which they worked were as follows:

Other personal services $24,780

Retail trade   24,180

Social advocacy organizations   24,100

Professional, scientific, and technical services   23,670

Animals may need care around the clock in facilities that operate 24 hours a day, such as kennels, animal shelters, and stables. Caretakers often work irregular schedules, including evenings, weekends, and holidays.

Some nonfarm animal caretakers work part time.

For more info on having a Pet Sitting Business:

Pet Sitting Business Book: How to Start & Finance a Pet Sitter & Pet Daycare Home-Based Business

By Brian Mahoney

https://www.amazon.com/dp/1986374068

Animal Care & Pet Sitter Web Rolodex

Pet Care Insurance

https://www.petcareins.com/
http://petsits.com/insurance.htm

Certification Programs

http://petsitters.org
https://www.petsit.com/certificate
http://www.ccpdt.org/

Pet Sitting Software

https://www.timetopet.com/
https://www.petsitclick.com/

Wholesale Supplies

https://www.petwholesaler.com/
http://www.petmanufacturers.com/
http://www.kingwholesale.com/

http://petsmart.com

http://petco.com

How to get Free Money for Small Business Start up

https://www.amazon.com/dp/1951929144   Paperback

https://urlzs.com/ZamJw   AudioBook

Tax Preparation Business

TAX PREPARATION SERVICE
Business Overview

Start up cost: $200.00 - $10,000

Estimated Yearly Income: $40,000 - $100,000

Normal fees: Flat fee for Form 1040 preparation, plus additional fee for every attached schedule, $50-$100 per hour.

Average fee: Not itemized $176   itemized $273

Marketing/Advertising: Referrals, networking, ads in local publications and Yellow pages, direct mail, online classifieds, website. Organic SEO, YouTube, Google Ads, Flyers, business website, contact Asset Management companies.

Skills Needed: An interest in people and their financial situations, patience, excellent math skills, thorough understanding of tax laws and calculations.

Equipment needed: Computer, fax/printer/scanner, high speed internet access, phone, tax preparation software, calculator, reference manuals, insurance.

Home business potential: Yes

Staff required: None

Unexpected costs: Errors and omissions insurance, time and money for continuing education (annual updates are needed), software upgrades.

TAX PREPARATION SERVICE

Tax preparation is the process of preparing tax returns, often income tax returns, often for a person other than the taxpayer, and generally for compensation. Tax preparation may be done by the taxpayer with or without the help of tax preparation software and online services.

Tax preparation may also be done by a licensed professional such as an attorney, certified public accountant or enrolled agent, or by an unlicensed tax preparation business.

Because United States income tax laws are considered to be complicated, many taxpayers seek outside assistance with taxes (59.2% of individual tax returns in 2007 were filed by paid preparers

Some states have licensing requirements for anyone who prepares tax returns for a fee and some for fee-based preparation of state tax returns only.

The Free File Alliance provides free tax preparation software for individuals with less than $58,000 of adjusted gross income for tax year 2010. People who make more than $58,000 can use Free File Fillable Forms, electronic versions of U.S. Internal Revenue Service (IRS) paper forms.

TAX PREPARATION SERVICE

What Bookkeeping, Accounting, and Tax Preparers Do

As organizations continue to computerize their financial records, many bookkeeping, accounting, and Tax Preparers need to use specialized accounting software, spreadsheets, and databases.

Bookkeeping, accounting, and Tax Preparers produce financial records for organizations. They record financial transactions, update statements, and check financial records for accuracy.

Duties

Bookkeeping, accounting, and Tax Preparers typically do the following:

Use bookkeeping software, spreadsheets, and databases

Enter (post) financial transactions into the appropriate computer software

Receive and record cash, checks, and vouchers

Put costs (debits) and income (credits) into the software, assigning each to an appropriate account

TAX PREPARATION SERVICE

Produce reports, such as balance sheets (costs compared with income), income statements, and totals by account

Check for accuracy in figures, postings, and reports

Reconcile or note and report any differences they find in the records

The records that bookkeeping, accounting, and Tax Preparers work with include expenditures (money spent), receipts (money that comes in), accounts payable (bills to be paid), accounts receivable (invoices, or what other people owe the organization), and profit and loss (a report that shows the organization's financial health).

Workers in this occupation engage in a wide range of tasks. Some are full-charge bookkeeping clerks who maintain an entire organization's books. Others are accounting clerks who handle specific tasks.

These clerks use basic mathematics (adding, subtracting) throughout the day.

Bookkeeping, accounting, and Tax Preparers use specialized computer accounting software, spreadsheets, and databases to enter information from receipts or bills. They must be comfortable using computers to record and calculate data.

TAX PREPARATION SERVICE

The widespread use of computers also has enabled bookkeeping, accounting, and Tax Preparers to take on additional responsibilities, such as payroll, billing, purchasing (buying), and keeping track of overdue bills. Many of these functions require clerks to communicate with clients.

Bookkeeping clerks, also known as bookkeepers, often are responsible for some or all of an organization's accounts, known as the general ledger. They record all transactions and post debits (costs) and credits (income).

They also produce financial statements and other reports for supervisors and managers. Bookkeepers prepare bank deposits by compiling data from cashiers, verifying receipts, and sending cash, checks, or other forms of payment to the bank.

In addition, they may handle payroll, make purchases, prepare invoices, and keep track of overdue accounts.

Accounting clerks typically work for larger companies and have more specialized tasks. Their titles, such as accounts payable clerk or accounts receivable clerk, often reflect the type of accounting they do.

TAX PREPARATION SERVICE

The responsibilities of accounting clerks frequently vary by level of experience. Entry-level accounting clerks may post details of transactions (including date, type, and amount), add up accounts, and determine interest charges. They may also monitor loans and accounts to ensure that payments are up to date.

More advanced accounting clerks may add and balance billing vouchers, ensure that account data are complete and accurate, and code documents according to an organization's procedures.

Tax Preparers check figures, postings, and documents to ensure that they are mathematically accurate and properly coded. For smaller errors, such as transcription errors, they may make corrections themselves. In case of major discrepancies, they typically notify senior staff, including accountants and auditors.

TAX PREPARATION SERVICE

How to Become a Bookkeeping, Accounting, or Tax Preparer

Most bookkeeping, accounting, and Tax Preparers need some postsecondary education and also learn some of their skills on the job. They must have basic math and computer skills, including knowledge of spreadsheets and bookkeeping software.

Education

Employers generally require bookkeeping, accounting, and Tax Preparers to have some postsecondary education, particularly coursework in accounting. However, some candidates can be hired with just a high school diploma.

Training

Bookkeeping, accounting, and Tax Preparers usually get on-the-job training. Under the guidance of a supervisor or another experienced employee, new clerks learn how to do their tasks, such as double-entry bookkeeping. In double-entry bookkeeping, each transaction is entered twice, once as a debit (cost) and once as a credit (income), to ensure that all accounts are balanced.

TAX PREPARATION SERVICE

Some formal classroom training also may be necessary, such as training in specialized computer software. This on-the-job training typically takes around 6 months.

Licenses, Certifications, and Registrations

Some bookkeeping, accounting, and Tax Preparers become certified. For those who do not have postsecondary education, certification is a particularly useful way to gain expertise in the field. The Certified Bookkeeper (CB) designation, awarded by the American Institute of Professional Bookkeepers, shows that those who have earned it have the skills and knowledge needed to carry out all bookkeeping tasks, including overseeing payroll and balancing accounts, according to accepted accounting procedures.

For certification, candidates must have at least 2 years of full-time bookkeeping experience or equivalent part-time work, pass a four-part exam, and adhere to a code of ethics.

The National Association of Certified Public Bookkeepers offers the Certified Public Bookkeeper (CPB) certification. To obtain the certification, candidates must pass the four-part Uniform Bookkeeper Certification Examination.

TAX PREPARATION SERVICE

Advancement

With appropriate experience and additional education, some bookkeeping, accounting, and Tax Preparers may become accountants or auditors.

Important Qualities

Computer skills. Bookkeeping, accounting, and Tax Preparers need to be comfortable using computer spreadsheets and bookkeeping software.

Detail oriented. Bookkeeping, accounting, and Tax Preparers are responsible for producing accurate financial records. They must pay attention to detail in order to avoid making errors and recognize errors that others have made.

Integrity. Bookkeeping, accounting, and Tax Preparers have control of an organization's financial documentation, which they must use properly and keep confidential. It is vital that they keep records transparent and guard against misusing an organization's funds.

Math skills. Bookkeeping, accounting, and Tax Preparers deal with numbers daily and should be comfortable with basic arithmetic.

TAX PREPARATION SERVICE WEB RESOURCE GUIDE

.National Tax Training School

https://www.nationaltax.edu/

https://www.ashworthcollege.edu/

TAX SOFTWARE

https://www.freetaxusa.com/

https://www.sigmataxpro.com/

Rated top tax software by PC Magazine 2020

https://turbotax.intuit.com/

https://www.hrblock.com/

https://www.taxact.com/

https://www.taxslayer.com/

How to get Free Money for Small Business Start up

https://www.amazon.com/dp/1951929144   Paperback

https://urlzs.com/ZamJw   AudioBook

Use YouTube to send traffic to your website for free! To learn more "how to"details use the link below.

"How to make money on YouTube"

https://www.amazon.com/dp/1795585439

Vending Machine Business

Vending Machine Business Overview

Start-up Cost: $2,000-$20,000
Potential Earnings: $25,000-$40,000

Typical Fees: $100-$500 per machine, less % of sales to the owner of the site.

Advertising:

Zero Cost Online Marketing, Internet Marketing, Business Cards, Classified Ads, Yellow Pages, Online Yellow Pages, Website, Referrals, Direct Mail Postcards, Business Groups

Qualifications:

Excellent sales ability, working knowledge of vending machines

Equipment Needed:

Vending Machines and Products being sold

Home Business Potential: Yes

Staff Required: No

Hidden Costs:

An average of 10 percent on what you earn from each machine goes to the property owner.

Vending Machine Business

Vending Machine

A vending machine is a machine that dispenses items such as snacks, beverages, alcohol, cigarettes, lottery tickets to customers automatically, after the customer inserts currency or credit into the machine. The first modern vending machines were developed in England in the early 19th century and dispensed postcards.

History

The first vending machine in the U.S. was built in 1888 by the Thomas Adams Gum Company, selling gum on New York City train platforms. The idea of adding games to these machines as a further incentive to buy came in 1897 when the Pulver Manufacturing Company added small figures, which would move around whenever somebody bought some gum from their machines. This idea spawned a whole new type of mechanical device known as the "trade stimulators".

Mechanism

After paying, a product may become available by:

the machine releasing it, so that it falls in an open compartment at the bottom, or into a cup, either released first, or put in by the customer, or   the unlocking of a door, drawer, or turning of a knob.

Vending Machine Business

Some products need to be prepared to become available. For example, tickets are printed or magnetized on the spot, and coffee is freshly concocted.

One of the most common form of vending machine, the snack machine, often uses a metal coil which when ordered rotates to release the product.

The main example of a vending machine giving access to all merchandise after paying for one item is a newspaper vending machine (also called vending box) found mainly in the U.S. and Canada. It contains a pile of identical newspapers. After a sale the door automatically returns to a locked position.

A customer could open the box and take all of the newspapers or, for the benefit of other customers, leave all of the newspapers outside of the box, slowly return the door to an unlatched position, or block the door from fully closing, each of which are frequently discouraged, sometimes by a security clamp.

The success of such machines is predicated on the assumption that the customer will be honest (hence the nickname "honor box"), and need only one copy.

Vending Machine Business

Bulk candy and gumball vending

The profit margins in the bulk candy business can be quite high – gumballs, for instance, can be purchased in bulk for 2 cents a piece and sold for 25 cents in the US. Gumballs and candy have a relatively long shelf life, enabling vending machine operators to manage many machines without too much time or cost involved. In addition, the machines are typically inexpensive compared to soft drink or snack machines, which often require power and sometimes refrigeration to work.

Many operators donate a percentage of the profits to charity so that locations will allow them to place the machines for free.

Bulk vending may be a more practical choice than soft drink/snack vending for an individual who also works a full-time job, since the restaurants, retail stores, and other locations suitable for bulk vending may be more likely to be open during the evening and on weekends than venues such as offices that host soft drink and snack machines.

Full-line vending

A full-line vending company may set up several types of vending machines that sell a wide range of products. Products may include candy, cookies, chips, fresh fruit, milk, cold food, coffee and other hot drinks, bottles, cans of soda, and even frozen products like ice cream.

Vending Machine Business

These products can be sold from machines that include coffee, snack, cold food, 20-oz. bottle machines, and glass-front bottle machines. In the United States, almost all machines accept bills with more and more machines accepting $5 bills. This is an advantage to the vendor because it virtually eliminates the need for a bill changer. Larger corporations with cafeterias will often request full line vending with food service.

Trends

In the late 1990s and early 2000s, there was a trend in the U.S. for large national retailers to have contracts with the national vending companies to provide full line vending services to all their branches' lunch / meal rooms. In most cases, managers and staff of individual stores objected to this, because the national vending companies were not necessarily responsive when making the product choices for the machines. As a result, this trend began to reverse. Most full line vending operators are independent and are small operations.

Often, they can have the existing vending machines removed and get permission to install their own machines by promising to lower prices, stock the machine with the manager's favorite candies, or provide better service (e.g. servicing the machine the same day if a coin jam or bill validator becomes jammed).

Vending Machine Business

Business description

For operators, soda/snack machines have the advantage that many locations recognize the need for such machines. Many locations will, in fact, take the initiative to contact a vending company to request installation of a machine. Moreover, companies recognize the difficulty in moving these machines and are less likely to request removal, unless the operator does a poor job of servicing the machine. Almost all soda and snack machines have vend counters that track how many items are sold, making it difficult for an employee to steal money. The machines themselves, being large and heavy, are difficult to steal without drawing attention, compared to most bulk vending machines.

Soda and snack machines are relatively expensive, unless they are obtained through a third-party vending program. Compared to bulk vending machines, full line vending machines take a long time to service – as much as an hour for a soda machine that is low on inventory. The product also tends to take up more space.

Breakdowns are difficult to repair, due to the complexity of the machines; do-it-yourself repairs may void the warranty. The machines are difficult to move; this task may require the help of professional movers. Moreover, some locations expect a commission.

Vending Machine Business

Nature of the business

There are many types of machines available. One type is the combo machine that sells both sodas and snacks. These combo machines have the disadvantage of not holding much of any product, and therefore requiring frequent servicing. Most operators use separate snack and soda machines.

Finding a good location can be difficult, since many locations already have vending machines, don't want one, or are too tiny to get enough business. An operator may end up paying the store owner a 10% commission, which requires separate accounting for that machine. If the locations are too far apart, the operator may spend so much time driving between locations when filling them that the same amount of time could more profitably be spent working for someone else.

Vendors occasionally enroll in a "charity program", in which the vendor makes a monthly charity donation in exchange for displaying stickers supporting the chosen charity.

Some vending machines are too heavy to carry without special equipment and/or helpers, especially if the machine has to go up or down stairs. As with bulk vending, turnover of accounts (in the event of a store closure or relocation, for instance) requires a repeat of the process of finding a location and moving the machine. Snacks and soda also have lower gross margins than bulk candy. Attention must be paid to the expiration dates on potato chips, sodas, and other products.

Vending Machine Business

The flexibility of a bank in handling coins is an important consideration when choosing the business' financial institution. A bank may not want a bucket of coins, so it may be necessary to find another bank or use machinery to organize coins into rolls. The government will expect taxes, tax forms, tax recordkeeping, and a business license.

Specialized vending

From 2000-2010, specialization of vending machines became more common. Vending extended increasingly into non-traditional areas like electronics, or even artwork or short stories. Machines of this new category are generally called Automated Retail kiosks. The trend of specialization and proliferation of vending machines is perhaps most apparent in Japan where vending machines sell products from toilet paper to hot meals and pornography, and there is 1 vending machine per 23 people.

In November 2013 online auto retailer, Carvana, opened the first car vending machine in the U.S. located in Atlanta.

Vending Machine Business

In schools

In schools, healthier vending options have gained popularity in the US. Such "healthy vending machines" are marketed as allowing students to perform better in addition to better health.

There has been debate over schools providing condoms for student use, possibly through a vending machine. In late 2012, 22 public high schools in Philadelphia installed vending machines providing free condoms.

United States

The United States is home to the most vending machines in the world, with over 6.9 million present. They generally sell drinks and snacks, although many, especially in grocery stores, provide DVD and Blu-Ray rentals through services like Redbox.

When starting out, one solid strategy is to go after the big factories and large businesses.

For more information on Vending Machine Startups:

https://www.amazon.com/dp/1539315932

Web Wholesale Resource Rolodex

Vending Machine Supplies

http://www.wholesalevendingproducts.com/

http://www.bulkvendingdepot.com/

https://urlzs.com/TvjhA

http://organicwholesaleclub.com/vendingmachines.html

Wholesale/discount vending machines

http://n.stuccu.com/s/Vending%20Machines

https://goo.gl/nZktF8

https://goo.gl/5fkQMS

FOOD

http://www.dollardays.com/wholesale-food-pantry.html

http://www.dutchvalleyfoods.com/

http://www.primafoodsinc.com/wholesale_food_distributor.asp

$10,000 Massive Money Internet Marketing & Copy Writing & SEO Course & $1,000 Value Bonus

Internet Marketing Videos

LIBRARY I (Video Training Programs)
1. **Product Creation**
2. **Copy Writing & Payment**
3. **Auto Responder & Product Download Page**
4. **How to start a Freelancing business**
5. **Video Marketing**
6. **List Building**
7. **Affiliate Marketing**
8. **How to Get Massive Web Site Traffic**

LIBRARY II (Video Training Programs)
1. **Goldmine Government Grants**
2. **How to Write a Business Plan**
3. **Secrets to making money on eBay**
4. **Credit Repair**
5. **Goal Setting**
6. **Asset Protection How to Incorporate**

$10,000 MegaSized Internet Marketing & Copy Writing & SEO Course & $1,000 Value Bonus

Library III
1. SEO SIMPLIFIED PART 1
2. SEO SIMPLIFIED PART 2
3. SEO Private Network Blogs
4. SEO Social Signals
5. SEO Profits

Bonus 1000 Package!
1. Insider Secrets to Government Contracts (PDF)
2. 1000 Books/Guides (text files)
3. Vacation Discounts (text file w/links to discounts)
4. Media Players (3 Software Programs)

100% MONEY BACK GUARANTEE!!!
ALL ON A 8 GIGABYTE FLASH DRIVE

This Massive Library with a $10,000 value all for only a 1 time payment of $67!!!

Get Instant Access by Using the Link Below:

https://urlzs.com/p7v3T

Leave a review and join Our VIP Mailing List Then Get All our Audio Books Free! We will be releasing over 100 money making audio books within the next 12 months! Just leave a review and join our mailing list and get them all for free!

Just Hit/Type in the Link Below

https://urlzs.com/HfbGF

www.ingramcontent.com/pod-product-compliance
Lightning Source LLC
LaVergne TN
LVHW012113070526
838202LV00056B/5723